U

N

R

A

V

E

L

BOOKS BY TOLU OLORUNTOBA

*Each One a Furnace*
*The Junta of Happenstance*
*Manubrium*

# Unravel

*Poems*

## Tolu Oloruntoba

McClelland & Stewart

McClelland & Stewart and colophon are registered trademarks of
Penguin Random House Canada Limited.

The authorized representative in the EU for product safety and compliance
is Penguin Random House Ireland, Morrison Chambers, 32 Nassau Street,
Dublin D02 YH68, Ireland, https://eu-contact.penguin.ie

Published simultaneously in the United States of America.

Library and Archives Canada Cataloguing in Publication data
is available upon request.

ISBN: 978-0-7710-1396-6
ebook ISBN: 978-0-7710-1397-3

Cover design by Jennifer Griffiths
Cover images: Portrait of Amenemhat III, ÆIN 924
Ny Carlsberg Glyptotek, Copenhagen. Image via ArchaiOptix /
Wikimedia Commons.
Typeset in Goudy Oldstyle by Sean Tai
Printed in Canada

McClelland & Stewart
a division of Penguin Random House Canada
320 Front Street West, Suite 1400
Toronto, Ontario, M5V 3B6, Canada
penguinrandomhouse.ca

1  2  3  4  5      29  28  27  26  25

Analyze. Attenuate. Audit. Break-down. Clarify. Collapse. Construe. Contradict. Corrupt. Crumble. Decipher. Decode. Decompose. Deconstruct. Decouple. Decrypt. Deduce. Degenerate. Demolish. Describe. Destroy. Detect. Deteriorate. Devolve. Disband. Disclose. Discorporate. Discover. Disembroil. Disencumber. Disentangle. Disintegrate. Disinvolve. Dismantle. Disperse. Dissect. Dissipate. Dissolve. Divine. Elucidate. Exegete. Exemplify. Explain. Explify. Expound. Finish. Free. Gut. Illuminate. Illustrate. Interrogate. Interpret. Invert. Investigate. Loosen. Luxate. Lyse. Pellucidate. Perlustrate. Probe. Prove. Puzzle. Ravel. Release. Resolve. Reveal. Reverse. Rewind. Rive. Ruin. Separate. Sift. Simplify. Solve. Spoil. Translate. Unbind. Unbraid. Uncoil. Undermine. Unmake. Undo. Unfix. Unfurl. Unhitch. Unknot. Unlock. **Unravel.** Unscramble. Unsnarl. Untangle. Untie. Untwine. Untwist. Unwind. Vitiate. Wreck.

# CONTENTS

## I

## II

UNRAVEL

I

I am the city falling into the sea.
But there remain acolytes in me,
singing in the cathedrals,
voices sanded with phlegm.
*Though he slay me, yet*
*will I trust him.* They are wrong
to trust me. If I know why
their world is ending, or why
it began; if I know the reason,
or the consequence of their lives;
if I know the spin-direction
of their dwindling cosmos,
I have not told them.
I have not revealed myself.

## CONTRONYM

to be both flammable and
*in*flammable, valuable and invaluable
is to understand that one can buckle
a thing down so it does not buckle,
can be a sharp stone under
the ravaging heel of gravity.
The way when I grow up I want to be
a choking hazard: one of the small
people clogging the airway of dominion.

I have raveled; have unraveled.
Have done and been undone.
To understand a name as meme
of control, a node of means I must
memoirize medics
who labored to excise each ill
by name—or outlines of one—
in the book.

Summoners who would Faust. Foist.
Hoist howls from hell.
Can I not be my own Antigonegonegone?
Holding a gnosis that pits me between gods
and men? Pit: a hollow, or solid,
at the center, or the membrane between village and villain.

The antagonyms of this language
trip me up. I was one in its long line of annexations,
then a wielder, welder in its concentrating camps.
Assimilated its murder charges, the spoils of its horde.

Locusts find a plant's tenderest loci;
they skin (that is, denude) the scaffold
above ground; they skin (that is, they clothe)
the scaffold above ground. What they leave,
even living, will go to fungi.

Sporulate. Diaspora.
The swell of an organism in decay,
launching probes is a final quest
for dispersal. Something of itself
wants to persist. *There*'s another reason
to have lived in a decade of cities.

Yes, I'm part of the saprophyte bloom
of a ripe and roadside body. So what?
Colonist spores settle, restless,
against the winds, then unfurl their children.

Human. Humor. Is the neutered animal neutral
-ized, nurtured, neither? Person. *Personne.*
Bound to one destiny, bound for another,
ambivalent.

I owned the only language I ever learned
to pray in, before I knew what it was.
*Let your words be few.* I used to bring
ugly phrases to the monolithic question.
I feared the similarity of *do* and *do not.*
Koan. Kháos. Inchoate. Hear,
here my cry. But we must speak
different dialects than Agnostos Theos.

We hold cards in the union of brave and dead
prison revolts. The warden had had inmates
carve our character with sharpened toothbrushes.
And we were made to make
our own graves, and those of the ones
who mean it all to us. And we had done monstrous,
shameful things to survive. But only ever solved
the large problems in assembly. So what must we do
now, before the gate that ends our death march?
Alas my contronyms must be a babble,
and untranslatable, to you.

A camel, ferrous brown—shoes sharpened
to crampons—may be ideogram enough, needle enough
to pierce the left wall of wilderness sentience. Holdfast,
hold, fast, through the breach.
The one we must confront awaits.

We're not going anywhere. If we were,
the towers we build against heaven,

idling like rockets receiving coolant,
or fuel, would've taken us to new worlds.

Towers must be the answer; the reason
God famously said: Let us bust their union.

Our Babel is fading into the American
we all speak now

in unclear silos, subdued
by the reptilian screams

of espresso machines. Cometh now
a new Nimrod: to captain our ships,

to find God for us on an evening stroll
elsewhere. And ask them some questions.

*Not to be removed until*
*delivered to the consumer.* "This,

is my body," Mimi the well-loved
seems to say in cruciform repose.

Someone had had to have
put the *dol-* in pareidolia, the barn

of polyester into you, many Easters
ago. You, like I, know the dolors,

the corruptibility of the self. Cheeks blued
and finger-printed, scalp pocked

with fingernails, mouth packed
with arcane detritus. I intone

the apocryphal writing on your face:
*talitha, kumi.* The modeling clay

and food oils caked on fig-bush
eyelash fall, like scales, like spit

-and-mud poultices for opening visions.
I lift you reverently to inspect, worshipful,

to listen to your sacred, plastinated heart.
Your eyes drop open.

A PARABLE

When the people asked,
*what must we do to be saved?*
the prophet said:
you want to be sure
the murderers hate you.
When those who play
marimba with bombs
on hamlets     smother the lights & aim their turrets,
their hatred must be white-
phosphorus-hot toward you, too,
because you have hampered the tank
thread with your body, you have
sandbagged your neighbor's house
from shellfire, you have
sabotaged the plant
where biomass undesirables
generate the genteel fuels of empire,
because they are coming
to your name too,
after the others.
Rejoice
if you are the one detested
because you, bollard,
did not let the settlement,
self-organizing witness
around defiant
olive trees, scatter. Because you knew:
if you were spared because
you did not protest the death squads,
you were one of them.

When the people heard this,
they went away sorrowful because
they had great goodwill with the captains,
and much indeed, more than their neighbors,
to lose.

HERE'S HOW I KNOW DISNEY'S *FANTASIA 2000*
IS A HORROR STORY:


Everything is coda in a never-ending world.

And the possibility that I am, myself,
endless, or not, is a terror.

Here, in the laboratory
of metaphysics, ax heads and
recombinant monsters float

from the beaker. My research lives
in nuclear notebooks. I have come
with questions for my maker,
fallen as I am, for astronomical units,

through the trapdoors of my request
for the genealogy of God.
I have stared into the galaxies
between the words of seers.
And I do not mean to presume,

or impose, but my arithmetics,
as given, are wanting
to seep through the page
into the supernovae beneath
where the answers,
veiled from our eyes, await.

When I disrupted the tomb, chiseling through
the stylized eyes and petrified shroud,

Atlantic sand had elided what glyphs would have
suggested a millennial birthdate for the child.

Pheasant birds lead-lined the opposite wall against
the final destruction of pith helmets; calling

papyrus down the Nile and vivifying the arms holding
the gold stool. To guard the hunter, a heart was left

in the body. Rapid eye movements had been crusted over
with igneous rheum and the privation of light.

I percussed the barrel chest, and its ampulla of skin, for speech.
Because resurrection is only for the dead—and he is *not dead*,

*only sleeping* in filigreed dysphoria—I am always back here
measuring the chamber in Vitruvian cubits.

I read the notes he'd left for me under the sarcophagus lid
before his lifeless and deathless nap.

What do I mean, what did I mean, where was I meant
to go? Why am I a coil of trouble, riposte waiting,

avenging myself? My Egyptology is only dissembling,
also a stratagem, a death mask for my frightened face.

I sidled my inner way to the stirring child.
I sat with him in the dark.

Urbino. I do not understand
the bar attendant because
I speak the imperial language.
She does too, after a fashion.

Wrong century, though.
Had this been 1480 I'd
have needed the other Latinate
scavenger on my tongue, under
the shadow of Mussolini's duke.

The palace. Federico is all bluster.
His 6 battles. His 8 victories.
His tapestries and wood panels.
The portraits showing his good

side. The books he made sure
to be seen reading. Funny
whose 15th-century palaces
have been allowed to stand

for civility and artistry. It's all negative
space to me, a sound without echo
across the Mediterranean. My brass
galleries are lost to the British cannon.

So I must view what is here in terms
of what is not elsewhere. *Ecce Agnvs Dei.*
It is revelatory to see whose blood was shed
for worlds past and present, who salvation

was for. Historians know art is all political.
See the cameos and guest appearances.
How many annunciaziones with Easter
eggs in them? How many counts seated

at the right hand of Christ?
I therefore view this art in the light
of its significance: the dark arts
of whitewash by artistic patrons.

I see why the fascisti loved all of this,
having brought Raphael's *La Muta*
back to his, and her, hometown.
In the wood-paneled studiolo,

Federico's hall of fame,
28 smug men looking down. I'm sorry but
allow me to despise these guys.
Who are they again? And how does one say

*This interpretation is not mine?* Have the back office
send a minority report. Tell me of the lone figures
in the background trudging uphill,
burlap sack on mule, dog behind.

Every *Profilo di imperatore Romano*
has villani—with no time
for the tragedies or ecstasies
in the foreground—as subplot: burdened,

unwinding their paths upward and forward.
They tend as always to make their way
right into me, way ahead of the saints
and their gods.

I'd always been
alarmed by the cruelty
of the parable of the fig tree.
But someone else had cursed you
before you got to me on a tray, unwoven
and pruned your roots, stunted you for the
T&T I bought you from. In the stories, people
tend trees as proxies for life. I did try. To cultivate
life, that is. See if it could survive outside of myself,
and therefore, within. My dear experiment. I could not
water you enough, or little enough. I had no secateurs like
the ones the nursery you came from amputated your limbs
with. I returned bushels of your leaves for a blanket, thought
I'd share my coffee grounds with you. I wondered about liquid
fertilizer, forgot the foods prescribed for your constricted throat.
I thought the remains of the coastal day centering the house could
nourish you enough. And thought the critical care of sun, light on the
balcony, would revive you. But it was winter, and already too late. Did I
place, or
abandon
you out
there?
Think
the rain would do my work? That the matches of meteorites would give
you nitrogen? That you would fade into the light pool out back? And why
do people plant children? I only know that once, you were the answer. I
used you to cultivate a laterite earth. Others, too, had young disallowed
to grow, smothered by droughts of bright, contorted, deceived, and frozen
in their reach for it, before the pruners took their sprouts of will. I wanted
the same ornamental achievement for you, like many parents tend to.
Dead ficus, can I blame you for not bringing leaves? Still, I have not
let you rest. A conspiracy of algae is covering or cradling your roots
now. I questioned my joy when I got you: was I broken or finally whole?

The spirit child's human father, today, would've tried to rise
in underground fight clubs, seeking money with a raccoon eye,

a black tiger's welts. Hunter-forager, the caves of his eye-sockets
would be painted with hemoglobin. There are those who wrestle

against tetramorphs with many-angled faces in constant feint,
and prevail. But like most workers, the boxer would be expected to
     throw

fights for payday, his body inventing an agrarian society, domed knots
of hamlets rising nightly, salting fields, irrigating the slashes of
     ploughing

knuckles with sweat. There are those who wear the chokehold of
     economy
as neckties, or necklaces. But why climb the pyramid, or blast the
     mine,

of bodies? Some swear the seed of life, and death, lurks always already
inside the thing, blood feud from the thicket curse of the earth. Earth:

substrate of all bodies, all societies, damned with spoiler quarks. Build,
then, fighter. Punch down your ziggurats. Ox-kick the axle pricks.

You were your own turnstile, receiving bus cards to daily austere
     offices,
the arm choking you in the bus seat, picking your pocket, your own.

When Kola Onadipe wrote of beings
that walked on their heads, he was describing
the anti-Mercator projection, the Alkebu-Lan
view of Africa, Xhosa cape in the north,
Habesha horn a tail.

You'd consider that map
upside-down, but only because
you believe Europe belongs on top.
This world is vertiginous at first,
where we were never punished

for speaking vernaculars, then punished
as adults for not speaking them:
exiled before our exile.
Akwaaba, hackneyed Ubuntu even,
meant we did not always assume

the treachery of merchant raiders;
that as payment for his Pahouin tour guides,
Conrad libelled them into a simple froth
on the banks. Dr. Livingstone, I presume,
did his share and we were indeed discovered

like so much termite food.
Somehow, Malaria didn't kill them all,
We bartered Nsibidi to appear unlettered.
Like elsewhere, for want of a mirror,
we welcomed the hemlock, the leprous handshake.

When that gravity of conquest is inverted,
don't laugh at *we wuz kings*. We could have been,
monarchs of ourselves, camelling to universities in
Timbuktu, Kano, the industries of Ilé Ifẹ̀,
with long shadows shading Europe for a millennium.

## OF PASSPHRASES STRONGER THAN 4 WORDS WITH 1,000 ITERATIONS

Society (or brain biology) would not simply give one
the combination phrase of happiness. I know
it exists because I have never cracked it.

Shrill bullets, sheep ballet, this hobble:
I still cannot pronounce shibboleth.
I wanted into the cult of ikigai like nothing

before or since. If I had been so punished,
then I must have been righteous, and my reward
must have waited.

Bhanu Kapil subjected me to (enhanced)
vertical interrogation: *Who are you and whom
do you love? Who was responsible for*

*the suffering of your mother? How did you arrive?
How will you begin? How will you live now?
How will you live now? How will you live now?*

I'd thought hatred would save me;
then I thought love would save me,
before I thought poetry would save me.

Piety did not save me either. My neural
alchemists were slovenly, their factory in ruin,
ringed by their disappearing industrial

product. To find a fluency of happiness
I must ask, therefore, who stopped the lathe
of language, and new kraals;

who made us transitional
between fires around where we're going,
and where we're from;

and why the earthworm,
exiled from its other half,
never stops reaching.

Some fishbone diagrams are planted head-down,
their cause-and-effect skulls becoming
roots in earths that like the whites inside of things.
The reds, too. Red herring. Herringbone. Bone
in throat. Throatbone. Some trees held the pulleys
that crushed hyoid bones of my relatives. It is only fair
that they eat what they killed. With their mouths slurping
underground, I hope they choke on avenging bones.
But I digress, as I do.

I am not the word *ramus*. I am the word *ramify*,
expansive with consequence. If there is no one
root of the problem that I am, and my roots, call them
predisposing factors, drape the shoreline in man-grove
stilts holding each other; and if the stems that appear
are conjoined at the waist, if the canopy is one
indivisible leaf the afro comb cannot tear; and I find myself
unsourced and non-destined, I can take, again, the moon's
flensing crescent and flay a nest of cobras from myself.
The snakes choose, chase, a water burial. My tree does not
point a direction; its direction is the sky. I'm a quiver
grown wide, undressed into the robe of sap
flowing into the water.

I cannot decide how to end this, but I

I was a misattribution at my physician's desk:
a false oath. Patients thought me an oracle

in those rooms. I, who had fled from
the smithy's smelting tongs, who would flee again.

I was too warm behind the masquerade,
which hide the countenances of òrìṣà.

Legend told of traitors swallowed
into sudden-cracked earth, where Anubis

had spliced a lion, a crocodile, a hippopotamus.
Those fates may catch me yet, but I've been

slippery. And I *did* obtain some of their due.
Like Ifá priests would prescribe sacrifice—

I gave requisitions for tests; I asked blood
of my supplicants and fed them to dark MRIs.

I removed things from, or stabbed, things into them.
I pulled newborns through birth canals

and cracked elderly ribcages on their way out.
An angel of death and doctor on call

can be indistinguishable.
And I was obedient to the instrument

of my divination: my tablet with scrying formularies,
and repeated the doctrines of prognosis, or fortune,

or profession prescribed for me. Up to a point.
Tell the crying and soothsaying egbére,

who surely seek me for collection
that I left, had had to, to heal myself.

MY FATHER'S FEAR OF DEATH CALLS ME AT 2 AM HIS TIME.

I do not wish to answer but it calls me like the edge of a train platform, a magnet to my metallic blood. Waiting to fall asleep is like waiting for death. I will not follow willingly. Sleep must take me, if at all, in my sleep.

*If I die before I wake*, has always meant I fight. Waiting behind the darkened door is the angel wearing the many eyes of its prey. Dressed in talcum, my slasher could be Willie Willie decanted from 90s TV.

The father injury is still there. Pinging. What do you call a 40-year ulcer? A chancre with explosions, Jovian hurricanes. We call sores like that undermined; the ones with a denuded rim wider under than above: an advancing exit wound.

And how can I describe my personification of nightmares? The person whose alarm of footfall, and how easily he could extinguish me, I learned to watch for?

My name is Renounce. To suborn a prophet's fervor has been my work. And here are the only three poems I ever wrote:

1. God, how could you?
2. Dad, how could you?
3. World, how could you?
(You must ignore me if you can take no more of this.)

The revenge that I am grows old; serves dinner cold. It cannot live off the tips of spears. Sleep means I must stop my campaign, that a thing with power has hoisted me again, my muscles limpid, ragdoll-soft. Let the church say *no, man*. I'm staying awake.

I.

When, while circling the wild aurochs, that whirlwind of muscle and rage flung the tamer, how did their companions know to wait for the mortar of calluses to bind the thigh bone?

It took more than six weeks for needling time, and collagen threads, to mend the femur. Someone dragged their hands, or more than one lifted them to the cave. Another fetched a gourd shard of water, or foraged succulents. Margaret Mead did not actually call this the kernel of civilization, or medicine, or patience: that not leaving others to misfortune. But what does it matter?

Bodies are simple conveyances for the genetic imperative. And in those bodies, the fraying rope bridge, of the telomeres binding the substrate of life, begin to wick away as whitecoat technicians tuck strands in.

I added little to that canon in the ravaged country: chain gangs of intern doctors ventilating infants, for days, with bag and mask. Then came the humid burn ward, its paraffin-soaked third-degree bodies leaking plasma, and fly larvae. And then I sat by lantern removing straw fluid from fourth-stage abdomens; I was a manual chemo pump for end-stage breasts. I helped too little. I wouldn't call the shopping bag around the valium drip, infernal above the rictus of tetanus, civilization.

We are here by the kindness of gags for debriding gangrene. By way of caring for the hominid without teeth. By way of discovering the gluing tendency of honey for wounds, and its fermenting tendency into mead. By way of the sip, then the mellow forgetting—of the unraveling dressing.

II.

The superstitious agree: humans could (or perhaps should) not have
stumbled on metallurgy themselves. It was the angel Azâzêl, it was
Prometheus, it was Hephaestus, or it was Ògún Làákàyè, teaching
apprentices at his bellows.

We return to the question of how Inuit knew to mine the meteorite's
iron. Was it Ridley Scott's Space Jockeys that showed them, or History
Channel's Ancient Aliens, on lunch break from building the pyramids?

Ilé Ifẹ̀ skipped the bronze and reached for iron. The crucible steel of
the Norse sword Ulfberht was purer than it had any right to be. Was it
Odin, was it Ọ̀rúnmìlà, Anansi, or Enki, was it daimones whispering
at the elbows of the smiths?

Whatever, whoever it was, I cannot discover, or create my own mettle.
But I had an Iron Age once, smelted from an avalanche of teen age,
so it must be possible; which is to say: If there be any ore in my dust,
I welcome the fire.

III.

Our first invention had been imitative learning. New in the species
school, we needed some instruction. Take tools, for example.
Tailorbirds, sewing with spidersilks, illustrated the science of traps for
prey. We could not have known of the poke required, the thread
snaking through, the tug that brought it all together. Or the oil-dipper
motions of a chimpanzee's angling for ants, that we extrapolated to
fish. Weaverbirds showed how strands could form a sheltering barrier,
or else fabric.

At some point we learned the lesson of beavers too, in the utility of a
shallow pool after a dam. That other mammals milked for their young.
Magpies showed how to build a hoard of shine. Squirrels, not meaning
to, taught us to plant. We would have seen the mating dances of
peacocks, dogs in estrus, and the nurture of brood animals. So no,
*complex symbolic language* is not our sole province.

Tarsiers proved that one could die by the suicide of head on rock.
Rodents harvested for winter. Call it multiple discovery, or convergent
evolution, but termites, *and* bees, built the first cities. (We read their
monarchies wrong, it must be said.) Elephants lectured in funerary
mourning. We saw the wisdom of flock migration. We were not the
only ones with opposable thumbs; ours were just longer, to do much
more with what we learned: To find a tool, and to use it for another.
To gather the food, and store some away. To find lessons in defeat. That
the pack hunts prey better. And some burdens require helpers. Think
of cities as lairs, or nests, and build some to nurture your needy young.
And learn from more defeats than not.

So what do we have above the other animals? What taught us to love,
or betray love? (And no other species could have made murder, or
money.) What brought the confessional or narrative urge? In their

eternal stalemate, *Love is as strong as death.* We are strong as neither, are but humble vassals hurled in combat, a war in which we learned the secret of fire, and metal, and abstraction, and art in the cauldron of cultural learning, a pot for planting   our tree-felling technology.

IV.

Humbaba was wrong(ed) in the first of the resource wars. That guardian of cedar groves where un-owned bounty maddened man; watcher with a face that was a coil of visceral distress, a script to scry splendors in pocks of horror. He grew more monstrous in each encore of the men sharpening adzes by firelight, a fateful ranger launching warning stridors between the dense trees.

Phallic Gilgamesh: the cables of his neck, and the news of his want, overtook foes in the first hint of dominion, and regime change. His sign is ours: a gorgon head, a beard cleft; heraldic field of treeslopes afire, and bleeding bark-wounds rotating over extracting axes. We clipped the last forest. Angels must die.

v.

The Bison Supermarket of the Plains, with those whose lives it hid within it, was shut down by Europeans who exalted the beauty of the flat, now-plainer ground.

Thread, bow, strings, quiver, nick, arrowhead. Even the rattles, the glue, cups and tannins, were taken. Those who hid their lives in utensils of *Bison bison*, harvesting what seasoning, what meat and hides, what clothing, tipis, and tools they needed, called twice to the rapidly dwindling herd.

Some call that decision—of usurpers to abolish 200 bovine millennia, herding them off the cliff to build polyhedral monuments from the lives of others—civilization. Some descendants still accumulate, and hunt for sport, continuing that bellicose work.

Infinite giver, bison, bison, how many times did I call to you? The horizon stays darkened with infinite takers, centuries into our apocalypse. Give cure for the westward blight.

VI.

The opposable thumb to the eye, or throat bone, and the thrown arcs
of igneous rock, were early prototypes for disrupting, or remaking the
body. Our claymation is reinforced with titanium knees, surgical
plasticine snaked with pacemaker wires, heart stents, and insulin
pumps. We want to keep going, budding off, building, breaking down
sets. Even the concrete and thermosets do not sit for long. Perhaps it is
just as well that we've been disrupted from enjoying our undress,
unable to cure the brain. Our curse, or blessing is this secret distress,
the partiality to lethargy. BIOS was a program to stay the bionic hand.

VII.

The French taxidermists called their diorama *Lion Attacking a Dromedary*, with its Atlas lion nipping at the harried courier, and camel.

It is untrue that that imaginary Arab was north African at all. It is however true that the camel-lion-man taxidermy, in a Freudian slip off its mount, contains non-imaginary human bones.

Carnegie's Museum of Natural History, no stranger to displaying human remains consentless, would not have minded at the time, had they known. They had, after all, placed this man in the North African Mammals section, in the country where Ota Benga, other kidnapped African, was a zoo exhibit.

Curators are, 150 years after, surprised by the human remains they are left holding. Yes, people are often stunned by the inconvenient remains they have on their hands, of the unending imperium.

The graverobber barons tried to put stuffing in everything. They must have discovered, then squatted by, the Tswana warrior's spoiled grave, on the carpet of open skin they'd unzipped, harvesting a skull, and bones: *Homo furtum*. Their imagination, limited by tanning and mounting, flickered as they hid another skull in their caricature for Paris Expo, hoping to stun.

It is thus imaginable that everything, for some, could be an image for the god Mammon, for whom things are always worth more dead than alive.

DISMANTLE

I've been curing my confusion since birth. Flesh. Salt. Smoke.
Jerk. I disagree with the sedimentation of the world into
the trinity of genes, memes, and toxins, magnified.
Geologic time knew what to do with the plumage of t-rexes,

with primordial colors now lost us. Could it capture
the energy in our leavings, and carbon-based sadness?
Wanting to compute odds of safety on the planet,
I keep thinking of the plankton-to-pipeline pipeline;

not those lizards we think became petrol. Open the metallic
wrap of the present, and its styrene cradle. So many landfills,
where aluminum can slumber in 100-year countdown
on the bottom bunk. Cities lie above, in valleys that mountains

of compacted trash days make. Mine those. So much
could come of the 2-week round trips of train tickets;
14-month ropes, milk cartons that rest after 5 years,
and fishing lines that could bite the dust in 600.

The 7 human lifetimes of diapers thus seem appropriate,
somehow. What could the sludge that seeps beneath
the pile be becoming? In the unlikely event that there are
humans that survive us, what will the milkshake straws

of their oilrigs vacuum, to burn again? I have found comfort
in the non-infinity of garbage. The earth was always likely

to outlast us, and now, our misdeeds. The last enemy
that will be destroyed is death. But before that, styrofoam,

tinfoil, and reactor cores are forever.


II: CANKER

So who rightly called us scum on the fluid-slick pebble?
Our ambit is minuscule. We have sullied this marble, yes,
but we could besmirch much more. Think of a heart in a body,
a nucleus in a cell, or human inside the titanium machinery
of conquest. Think of the abandon, the colonial singularity
of our red goo. We may be feeble, algae, but our exoskeleton
grows interstellar, probing fingers bearing gifts of gold disks.
*Listen*, we say. *Kneel.*


III: POISON

And because we are enthralled by death,
the door we must negotiate,

I think of the boy milking himself at the end
of Pompeii, sky full of cinders,

and know you'll never disarm creatures
of their stingers.

The venom of adders, pressed to muslin,
is medicine in the right dose. But what dose?

In the next evolution,
our pupils have hollowed crates
for ring lights.

Band hands remember pillbottles.
Android sixth fingers are angled for
screen bevels.

There are discreet cranks for the brain.
Jet ejection clauses come standard:
an ability to excise one's

self from things.
Neither persistent gravity, nor affinity to others.
There are sharp elbows, olecranons grown long:

stabbing knives good for nicking kidneys,
or hands, of those that would hold you
back,

and tongues that no longer perceive
the dark taste of Hershey's
worker children.

Though the SSRIs in the tap water give us all
bleeding tendencies, the fluoride
will protect our gums.

Let the *why* repeaters in our heads fire
upon the *noli timere*
of soma choirs.

We cannot run without the hamstrings
we left behind, neither do we, sated,
know of a need to run.

The longing machine breaks lab animals to intuit
its own nature, seeking its lost and original build:
but there is consolation in the resonance

it finds in music, even in the singing stars it traces
other people into: the futile hunter, the doomed
beauty, the Never-ending Bear Hunt.

Its forces carry artist sketches of the person it needs
to find. It holds a fondness with its cargo.
It assigns a genus to each find: not this, not you, not like

this. The longing machine flexes the nautilus tail
of its amygdala. An engine-light loss winks on.
Thumbing the peepholes of portals, it murmurs,

*Are you it?* Are you them? Are you here      for me?
It knows you will miss the tells of person-thirst, like air-
hunger, if you did not learn the signs.

But sometimes combinations align and a poor fool falls
into devastating, slot-machine love.
The longing machine has sensed its own loneliness,

clenching the dream the sinkhole is taking;
its chassis tense after the voyage of sleep.
It has crossed borders for a shadow of likeness.

It happens on the chasms, the not-its between
atoms, facsimiles more absence than presence,
and the reason that its distress alarms

could never be hushed.

# ON WHETHER OR NOT THERE IS MARRIAGE IN HEAVEN

*SEPTEM PECCATA MORTALIA*

How far did we think we could jump? Even objects in low orbit, seemingly afloat, are constantly falling.

I am living in the afterlife of betraying my own will, cut down, burst open, spilling shekel moons.

How did our plant, neglected by my brown thumb, become carnivorous? Our thing did not die, it became hungry.

Our carnassial blades of chlorophyll did not mean to be cruel, or did they?

If I enter the undertow of toxins, the swing ride of poison fruit, will I collect an answer?

Do you still love me, you ask. Yes, I reply, as if I am lying.

The ship is taking on water. The ship is going down. The captain is staying on the ship. I am the captain. I am the ship.

\* \* \* \* \*

*NARCISSUM*

And speaking of slot-machine love,
despite my efforts all my vows have turned
into deceit, or tried to, does not matter.
My browser knows whom I love, or loved,

does not matter. It knows the secrets
of players who request another fortune,
who unburden the self into the infinite slat,

cursor frothing in the wake of douououououbt.
Browsers know how many times a day a name
is searched, willing something to have changed.
I am a failed experiment in integrity. F5. Refresh.
Refresh. Refresh.Refreshrefresh. *Are you there now?*

I am prone to gravity, and devastating falls. I feel
the acceleration of this illness, this frenzy toward
certain salvation. *In leghold traps, it is common*
*for an animal to chew through its leg*
*or paw to free themselves from a trap.*
What animal? A coyote, a wolf.
Apt, since one breaks people out of one home
into another, while the other, big-bad, breaks
the house for an inviting morsel.

One should not quote themselves
but I once said: *We have crucified our fathers;*
*we hope our sons will be kinder to us.*
I have daughters. And the Narcissus pool
has personified my ideal to me.
And I have paid with a sure infatuation.
And I will never have paid enough.

\* \* \* \* \*

PYGMALION

I love you
but I do not know you.
I love you
because I do not know you.
I love you
because I made you.
I know you
because I made you.
If I knew you
I would not know you.
If I knew you
I might not love you

or I might shatter.

\* \* \* \* \*

COLLAPSUS

There are ungrouted grooves where
my wanting waits.

I am alarmed by the hydraulic force
I have built into my grasp.

It could crush any mortal. I am the Cerberus
unfed for millennia, unsure

that this yearning is safe
for your approach,

but I need you to touch me.
My hunger has spawned other hungers

and digesting mouths,
but I need you to kiss me.

Is your scarab coat, too, hungry as I am?
How terrible is it for annulling forces

to seek the sizzle of solace
when all they have left        is that risk?

\* \* \* \* \*

MONSTRUM

And when my loneliness had grown ravenous, as in a raven, a ravine,
a ravaging, a pet wolf made of cuspid teeth, I realized my danger. I
wanted all who saw this to run from me; to run toward the damage of
my arms.

\* \* \* \* \*

PURGATIO

I'd tell Simic I don't know
if there are weddings in hell,
but here in limbus, we make our home.
I am Injury, prone.
Band triangle swings broke my wrists
on the first ride. I broke them again falling
from rafters of the school shed,

from the nail watching my Spider-Man lunge,
leaving a rail track reminder, stoplight-red.
The third was from a motorcycle
and the sheep avalanche crossing the road.
I don't go out anymore.

I was once unprepared for the sap writhing in me,
and the loggers waiting outside,
and the bright and unbearable reality
of limerent objects.
I try navigating a world that was a Rorschach
of kryptonite breasts, Eurocentric standards,
and a half-Romanian crossbolt
that set me to falling for six years.
I had not been warned.
I was driven insane by visions,
I was baton for my Pantheon of hunters:
the black hole, the twin Gorgons,
the cardiac clamp, and milky clasp.
To cure me of mad passions, see:
I've sworn off passion.

\* \* \* \* \*

ILLUMINATIO

I come to,
marooned on an unfamiliar love.
I've always conducted
lightning too easily, yet never expect it.
I glow inside my ribcage
after the strike.

I am contradiction.
My seasalt ankles have not
survived the tide.
I crouch now
before your judgement.
Like dog years,
poet years do not count the same.
The last two have been especially dog,
forgive me. The ordnance of my story
was good. A little too good.
The halls I built last month are
cordite already. I cannot linger.

Greedy for a cure,
I have long longed for the embrace
of strangers I see the light around.

I come to again climbing the mountain
just fast enough, its frost tongue reaching,
stirring the clouds,
my oxygen cylinders
already falling away
like rocket stages.
I long to linger,
but in the illogic of this dream,
I climb faster.

\* \* \* \* \*

I show, you show our affliction. We
who are at our most human when
we are yearning. My Cain-mark, your
Cain-mark, shows even, especially
in this gropesome dark. And because
longing is never satisfied, it takes a village
away, to have ours be so vulgar.
Saudade, sehnsucht are beautiful
only in theory. People need us
to keep the keening to ourselves.
Scientists found the four words
at the core of all our language:
"GOOD," "WANT," "BAD," "LOVE."
And we found belonging to be
the only bandage for longing,
we great apes who keep trying,
the kind of gambler
this casino loves.

## MATING IN CAPTIVITY

Our embrace keeps what is outside out,
and who is inside
within.

In this way arms
make for excellent cages,

and the safe deposit box—
that our muscles are braided taut over—
can hide keys that remain
unused in a cradle of rust.
I will not be the first

to point out the relation of *ally* and *alloy*,
and our bonding into a hardness
that could survive.
I will not be the first to show
the line between *diaspora* and *dispersion*

and the desolation of these latitudes
with their silent assemblies of sunflower fields,
and the madding hordes we fled from
too gone to wish back.
We had sought to become a grate

over the cracks people fall through
but freefall has been given a bad name.
Migrant workers ask their lovers
to be everything: a holy grotto, a dry bright
in the pacific north, a home that will survive

the big quake we have been expecting.
She was an invocation of sanctuary.
The poets have written *hiraeth* to death.
The longed-for past and country
are lacunae in space-time,

hiding where loose socks
and house keys do.
I am no different, I, too,
have left one home for a person
who could be universal,

larger within
than a person should be,
and arrived to the empty
all abstractions
are constructed around.

Astronomers have called this quandary,
that lost-and-found crate
at our galaxy's core
a supermassive black hole.
In that crash,

our quantum found some
not-thereness,
to superpose a thereness onto,
and we were once again
outside.

So can one want what one already has?
I am lying in a strange brook.
A sun, wearing her face,

is crying into my eyes.
Yes, I want to come home.

Not to the structure
we had welded ourselves into:
but a new and dangerous place.
Because true play is the death of bars.
And there is no safety in play.

1.     *Practice coping skills first to be ready to work on changing your nightmare*

      I am not uniquely evil.
      The things I did were human things.
      I am only as guilty as the rest of us.
      I stopped short of the final stroke.
      I have sought forgiveness.
      I am making amends.
      I also forgive myself.

2.     *Choose a recurring nightmare to work on*

      Lunacy is from the root word *luna.*
      Werewolves know both worlds well.
      I awoke after my rampage of greed.
      And I was naked, because I was afraid,
      and I hid behind the person,
      the proxy I gave to myself.
      I went upon my belly to sleep,
      to stopper my snoring with the dust
      mites I have I eaten all the nights hence.
      I dreamt a rawhide toga, a referral
      to lower courts of toil, and dying-tendency,
      radial angles of spinning lightsabers
      and avenging angels banishing me
      from the private property of god.
      I awoke on my back again, drowning
      in the water vapors of the room,
      and thirsty for a drink.

3.    *Write down your nightmare*

The dream
delivered on my worst fear:
that I could become,
or was becoming an omen.
May I be redeemed by my
horror at my trickster self. I plead
the logic of sleep paralysis
because I willed, without effect,
the quills back into my skin,
the claws into their sheaths.
Let the record show that I did
not want this. I did not
love to stab, but confess
that I loved the jade knives
my poisons had crusted into.

4.    *Choose a new outcome for the nightmare*

I defang myself before my final turn
into Calibos. But again, monster,
from *monstrum*, is to demonstrate.
A monster is a sign, a beacon.

5.    *Write down the full nightmare with the change*

What signal? That
if I was lunar I was
halfway between scintilla
and debris. I twirled, in phases,
to the musics of gravity.
I do not fight them now:

aphelion, perihelion,
Wolf Moon.

6.   *Each night before sleep, rehearse the changed nightmare and then*
     *practice relaxation exercises*

     Love may explode the brain's drug lab
     but let us surrender to the instincts of the animal
     the saltlick of the other's skin makes of us.
     The contractions of oxytocin an entrapment
     in a bond where it is safe,
     where I furnish our enclosure
     with atonement.

7.   *During the day, visualize the dream and practice relaxation techniques*

     There's a boat being candle-wicked downstream,
     the boat keel a tongue sounding the depth of water.
     Forgive me, I'd been carried away. Call me
     discoverer now,
     tell me where to go.

Who steers boats of bread, cast previously on many waters
in their return laps to us, spores fleeing the sails like distress flares

piloted toward a formally inventive drought? Downwind,
will the sky lanterns of fungal bloom crash on us

as our footfalls thresh—like Singer pedals—
the absence of seed on this shore?

Will our news come at last, our gaze vertically trashing;
laterally looming, weaving a hoist, a mast, an ensign?

If there is no fruit, return our kernels of effort.
Deliver landfall to us.

In this way is deathing a way of birthing: come to calve,
the doe of plasm arrives to deliver the spark it has unwrapped.

Allow some integrity to the zips of my body's bag, but if that fails,
deliver to the swaddling cosmos, the me that animated

this decomposing flesh. Collect it on a chain,
with the sthlurp of bios exiting the purse strings

that held my deflorescence. I have been
the death of the biosphere. And now Entropy

says to me: *be not proud, though some have called thee*
*Mighty and dreadful, for thou art not so*, but I already knew.

## ÀRÓSỌ̀ POETICA: A CENTO OF ARS POETICAS

I am very lonely.
if you can arrange it,
I want a piece of your mind,

your million names
Not for the doctrine but the music there
the birth certificates

hanging in stalks like votive offerings,
a three-dimensioned life;
with bags of rice strapped to its saddle.

"Consequence" is the word that splintered my mind
into excess and violence
Sometimes I tremble like a storm-swept flower,

to make my body in the world feel real,
Sometimes I feel
I've made my home in that motion

to transmute the outrage of the years
These lost and charnel thoughts
The pillage of cells, the language

Across a lascivious empire
Into five blades of light
but let's listen, spooning in the dark, for

Hush-throated nestlings in alarm
Linger there — it is quiet — your breath
I discard eloquence

into what I'll carry
Supple in the air, vague, flexible,
Because anything can be fixed. Praise you,

Poetry (here I hear myself loudest),
Six monarch butterfly cocoons
become a flight of birds

II

"You continue the gestures commanded by existence / the escape from
everyday sleep / in the face of the cruel mathematics that command
our condition / the chain of daily gestures

Everyday conversation feeds on / this ardor or these silences /

weariness has something sickening about it / The worm is in man's
heart / in the face of his universe / in the eyes of the absurd man /
a heavy yet measured step / A face that toils so close to stone

That revolt of the flesh / is the rock itself / the only bond linking
him to the world is the cool hand of a girl / the myriad wondering
little voices

bureaucrats of the mind and heart / tumble before / the wine of the
absurd and the bread of indifference / The important thing . . . is not
to be cured, but to live with one's ailments

Death, too, has patrician hands which, while crushing, also liberate /
At that subtle moment when man glances backward over his life /
at the end of the acts of a mechanical life / He is stronger than his rock

the body shrinks from annihilation / the clear vision he may have of
the / limited universe in which nothing is possible but everything is
given / the cry that terminates their itinerary

the fresh start with arms outstretched / There is no fate that cannot
be surmounted by scorn / in its distressing nudity / the privileged and
implacable visage / the wholly human security of two earth-clotted
hands / I leave Sisyphus at the foot of the mountain."

Production has continued. We have invented
the whitest of white paints, a shine to repel
the witness of the sun. Soon, it will adorn
townhouse complexes on boulevards where

the blades of hung windows await the neck.
With dollhouse greens and HOA beiges, these
are national cakes, and if you believe in such things,
also rewards, for the faithful. Beach houses

are the calcium levees of the excess dead;
the resourceful have found use for so many bones.
That they are sunk now like Archimedes means that
oceans must rise. The new marsh of color-coded

pickets will forbid sleep, even with lockjaw skin
on the duvet of morning. A penumbra,
an afterimage of tarp, and cardboard cities, lingers
around the opulence. After the pulse that repeals

electricity, some of us will still have IKEA train tracks
for wood, and crayons for candles. In that beginning,
foil blankets wrapping meat within, we will wait
for the shadow over our shadows to lift off

the high-thread-count embrace of sleep, hoping
to remain space-dark behind the taped glass
eyes, and cheekbone wounds, of our estate,
safe from our neighbors.

# SOFTWARE DEVELOPMENT LIFE CYCLE

I.

Builders of code pyramids are useless
when their work is done. Unrelated:
the chambers they build will always
need upgrades. The laser Horus eye

at the peak, asking sphingean riddles,
is insensible to all but a bad sacrifice.
In ergonomic cuffs, we ship haiku pleas
in charters and deliverables, fidget in

a persistent, post-shift near-dawn,
prophesy of the next project cycle,
a final widget to transform the
quotidian into new contracts.

We do not strive to interlope.
Great Eye, give us visas,
or do not. We must bring
our bottoms out of the cold.


2.

There were test environments before this
for flattening our names in preparation,
circumcising diacritics, rinsing ethnic slag
from journeyperson feet, certifying selves

for the excellent mopping of price floors.
A contrived imitation, a syrupy plea
is the pass for downtown. On the lam
from ghouls of inadequacy through monocrop

fields, we must paddle looms faster, work
the land we've baled brick in, feeding it daily
social security, with more diligence for our escape
afterward—into the wilderness of mirage

mead ahead, should we make it across.
In dreams of sugarcane, architects inverted
the labor of exiles into remittances. They wanted us
for scaffolding. We wanted nothing more.


3.

Lost in the cereal brush of downtown,
hordes of migrant harvesters walk the stalks,
scurry the sheaves and look,
through millet-head windows,

upon the world's unslaked thirst for carbs.
Do not ask why gluttons for hope worship
the chandelier sword of Damocles.
Countries whose turn it is

present their shiniest. Chain gangs return
with sweat offerings for gods of intention.
Their fatty fingers are prone to error
on the ballistic sequence, their windmills

grind no justice but they, glowing green
in the grove, hard disks an armor
against the vines, are holy.
You are one of us now.

Do not seek the door.
Approach the idol in the alcove.

If L = λ x W, the engineers of our Trolley Problem
need people to shovel their coal. I did all I could
to become one of those consultants. But having seen
the lethality of PowerPoint bullets, I'm glad I failed.

Business school had taught me to calibrate the velocity
of mincemeat supply chains, but in an ethical, non-Enron
way. I learned to say *meritocracy* with the right
jackknife inflections; to say *maximize* with canines mincing

lifers into part, short, and no-time workers. I learned
to say *optimize*. Little's Law smoothed the queues
loading train cars, and path to engineer. I could,
meanwhile, inventory people to the bottomline rail,

and one diverging track. For science, or the economy,
I'm not sure which. I hold no illusions
of virtue. In Mesopotamia I would have been a scribe
of empires, chiseling reports, writing staff manuals.

I am not, I'd have told myself, a toenail remover,
or executioner, just a hard worker keeping his head
down, not discussing politics at work, especially the politics
of that work. Revolutionary poetry, or pottery, though.

I'd make those by lamplight: containers for my guilt.
I would overhear news of popular uprisings, and refreshed
despots who need middle managers. The dams,
aqueducts, civil servants and the water they hold,

cannot be displaced. Those who seize the means of means must maintain them. I will never be out of the work I have not done. If we are 70% water, then the hydraulic empire is everywhere. And more importantly, it is forever.

Elsewhere in another time,
Ernesto Guevara left malarious.
Dead civil engineers in white
fish bellies bore witness
to the amphibious traders
who spoke in gestures of commerce
and built a city on deeper stilts
than Berger pylons.

Lagos and her money are seldom,
or never, parted. Her binary abacus
is weighty with zeroes.
In Abracadabra Bureau de Change,
you will gather the fundamentals:
that Allen boys chop your dollar
with sleight of hand. So laborers
on the pyramid scheme must die.

Megacity planners
will say, *Èkó ò ní bàjé.*
No, Lagos must not spoil,
because it is no place for
the illegal, the unbeautiful,
or unvigilant
once their bloods run
dry behind the pistons.

Investors must renovate
whoever does not fit the decor-
um, and paint them into the fences

of new estates before BBC
documentarians, or the investors,
can see. They are the mortar,
and the bedazzled waterfronts
that seduce you, the lie they hold.

The three elders will welcome you,
Tarkwa Bay will tell you the truth,
but Victoria is always, forever, fabu-
lar. Furtive birds of 6 am,
will recap your objectives
when you wake for work in traffic,
playing for oxygen;
inhaling deep for the plunge

into the city's burr holes—
with the black-and-yellow
of its sweaty-collar platelets
ever borne on slow tides
toward payday.
You may have heard
of the cashless economy,
meaning *you*, cashless.

What is the exchange rate
of old ambitions for new?
Or scratch paper
for Owó Èkó,
the once-won lottery
paid back in tuition, taxes, and tolls—
by those who think they can,
and who know they now must.

# I WAS GOING TO BUY A PARAKEET, BUT THE LAUNDROMAT LOST MY CLOTHES

By parakeet, I mean one of the books that speak to me
in recto and verso blurs round my head, a songbird self,
a voice I can bear to listen to. Call it budgerigar, its bungie
hook coos talking, then strapping me down. By *a* parakeet,

I meant *more* parakeets, levitating meathooks to halt my
freefall. Next time. I am more prone to helium jumps, and
osmium sways, and tightrope thoughts, now. Train platforms
remind me of fragility. The laundromat, with its MonFri spin

cycle, its dryer-sheet currency, called, taunted. The snap
of the door had scattered, again, the thread from my clothes
in sudden flocks of lint. I already knew. I had begun to sift
down onto the November sidewalk. I, like the fabric

of my clothes, emulating the down of my birds, no scaffold
of beaks and claws to hold my strange, human, snow.

## A GOOD REASON

In the space between molecules, an eddy,
a body of these; a scaffold of dissolving bones,

a terminal case of chaos. In the space between us,
winds of your young sun, the timelapse spokes

of our arms. And you don't know it yet,
but treading the water of space-time I've been asking

why we end, why eddybody you know today may fade
from your hearth. I mourn this even as the pulleys

of my frame flap, and my covalent bonds wander apart.
The equation for a loving deity demands

that our intricacy continues in some form.
What a waste, otherwise. Recycle me not fully.

Let some sentience remain. Beyond the needle eye
we all shrink from,

if it is at all possible to guard you here, to go,
and petition, for reason, for cure, I will.

# EKPHRASIS

## I: ATTENUATE

The land is helpless in its oceanic fist.
Diaphanous Aladuras in white are dogged
on their spent strip of Bar Beach where
disillusionments are acrid salt sprays
crashing into the sky.

I had been troubling
the shoreline,
as cryptids do.
Auditing consciences
had advised that the flour-
ishes of my desperation
had become baroque;
that I consider a-
gain the fill line of my muchness,
a cup-
rim for my storm.
Intransigent, I
had asked terra
infirma to give
hydroponic trees, log-
arithmic wood to print upon, to give
spare squids
for the inks I laid, laid over, laid again
into a curdling lattice for colossal feet:
staircase out of surf:
a giant causeway of entreaties:
a basalt typewriter to parkour my
story across.

My *help me*
was invocation,
dire glammer, binding
spell, prayer of salvage
from dissolution beyond boulders
that braced for the bite of the sea.
The pray-ers
on the beach could've been calling
for me, calling to my own gurgling
petition with cudgel arms raised,
breasts righteous, robes sinusoidal
in knowledge of the crests and troughs
of drums and song. And even if all that
was left of me was a darting eye in fishbowl,

I'd been rebuilt before.

Attenuate me not. Make me more myself,
a testament of krill greening my kill site,
life form profuse and boiling the shore in entry
as I cry out from my water rebirth,
and those who had believed, and waited, rejoice.


2: CONFESSION, CIRCUMFESSION, CONTRAFESSION

The pink mist of god
(assuming god explodes like a human)
is haunted by the mechanical ghost of god.

This one had been nice.
I'd subverted the imperious Baptist—
into the genial African of efferent locs

one could hide in, or ride upon—instead.
Unlike my own exemplar of our artful father
in heaven, this one had let children come near.

They'd sensed his refuge, the approachable
brooks of joy in his laughter,
and were radiant in elliptical orbit.

The wind clanged, then hushed the cymbal
pleats of their dresses and their sweat-shiny feet
told the grass giddy secrets. 20 children

cannot play forever but I'd expected these 6,
primary elements, to remain. I carried the warmth
of this chiral, surprising form of god, and the gravity

of his system, to the road. This one would have no lighting-
bolt whips, no judgement door to stand trembling behind
before opening, no testament of breaking. Such a deity

insisted, on being. This has been called faith,
by some. The cosmos, in the stage whisper it favoured,
insisted as well. As children do, I *became a question*

*for myself,* the force of my pounding queries shutting doors
that would open outward had weakened
the house of non-sequiturs. The dark made me chimera.

Speaking of his body Jesus had said, *tear down this temple.*
He would have wanted this explosion the father
was becoming with the speed of tectonic schisms,

frittered into obligate inconclusions: a *may-being.*
This has been called apostasy, by some. Truly,
to Deus Absconditus, we are the ones who chase

after winds of an unstable outline. Just past the gates
of blasphemy, nuance mudslides, and the menace
of thrones, I could have used another helper.

The fear that he hefted a shadow behind him—
he of the innumerable company of angels with eyes
whirring panoptic, and an endless murmur-

ation of wings, their mass bending light away,
their magnetism casting fearsome dragnets—
went with me. Because I,

and whatever man I could construct,
would always hold a necessary hollow.
I confessed I'd been a stone cast from the garden,

lonely, and tumbling. Although it had been true at the time,
I realized I could not know what I believed I believed,
or would do, when I said I did (I could say the same

of my marital vows, but I digress). This is the tragedy
of juvenilia. Out so long past curfew, so far from home,
I feel the heavy hand of wrath above me. I feel

a sense in my chest, a tensing as my muscles
*take my blood* as in communion, for flight. I am guilty
of something. I just do not know what it is. I wish

they would say. But parents do not always feel brave
when they must address their progeny, although I promise
I can be reasoned with. My gospel of roguishness,

disruption, and attention, will not harm you.
Because if I cannot be complete, but you choose to speak,
I can be with you, and beside myself.


3: THREE STUDIES FOR FIGURES AT THE BASE OF A CRUCIFIXION

The pelican is the bird of sacrifice. In my
anthropomorphic mouth, there are teeth
missing. My kerchief blindfold is on. It is,
after all, an execution, and my pedestal
is the gallows gravity will pull me from.
And if eyes be the window of the soul,
in these last moments, I hold my counsel
behind my skin-grafted mask. Should any
thing be seen, let it be the dorsum of my
kissed and anointed foot. The oil was
spikenard, I remember. My companions
on either side, one looking down, the other
unhinging upward from her continent,
are also the ash of murderous evenings,
stark against the muscle-orange sky.


\* \* \* \* \*


Gestas of the dismal howl has been maligned
unfairly. Trust churchmen to demonize her
as impenitent for her questions. She was guilty
only of this: not being fawn enough. Dismas

had done what we all would, try to snag the last
ticket beyond the molten embrace of his swaddling.
He knew I knew. He could not meet my eye.

* * * * *

Now the chiggers lining my veins are fleeing
from the hole in my side, in dark shafts down.
Run, darlings. Find another. Welcome
the *I will never know* I bequeath. In this triptych,
I cannot touch my friends across our plots of sky.
But the drool of our screams can seed the hill
with iron, and our roots can become global
in stealth escape from centurian gazes.
In this end, our illness is awake, awave again.
*Come*, it says. *Yes*, we say.

and *a thousand years are like a day,*
each day of each year in turn a thousand years long,
one could say the day on which man was created
was a thousand years long: a thousand years of days
each a thousand years long, ad infinitum. It is simplistic
to imagine a world created in 7 days, and not a yarn
of crocheted balls of yarn and a spiral galaxy animated
by a spiral galaxy of base pairs. The corkscrew serpents
of genetic material unspool into the multicellular profusion
that has, duly, subdued the earth. The nucleus is that bath
bomb made of bath bombs. If *All the days ordained for me*
*were written in your book before one of them came to be,*
and each of the 86,400 anvil seconds are on a ledger
of yours, how tightly must you pack meaning,
before I can find it?

Ambivalence is the most earnest prayer: *ambi + valere*
to be halved by two powers, one's mouth seeking
to coax the fire, the other's to blow it out. Come out,
we seem to plead, taunt. We just want to talk.
Evangelical Christians have a fear of the bottomless pit
soldered into them early. If, at the edge, you whispered,
screamed hoarse, *please be real*, your voice, voyager
to the other end of the expanding and multigalactic tube,
with the waterfall of infinity gushing on the other side,
would not return to you. God is wise to hide from us.
If we ever found god, we would have vivisected god
for some answers.

I BELIEVE; HELP MY UNBELIEF


The aftertaste of those who taught me love is wormwood.
Like we eat lamb, or veal: some diseases lunch on children.

They wipe the reason for this off their mouths, before I can see.
The holy hands above the lectern have held shut the latches

upon infants, and no times-table can compute the damage
of anointing oils on the water table. We must live with this:

to be unsettled by rust on the ripples, the bloody palm prints
of well beings on the capsized surface of plenty.

I have seen through the diastema of some pearly whites,
and the mere darkness beyond. But I grasped at some,

any Christ, my dissonance tolling through a dust bowl,
its peals making stars of silica and the soot that coats

my hollow. I suppose this is the puzzle of faith: the mitotic
Rubik's cube in a technicolor dream coatpocket, growing,

and losing a tail, new thumbs ascending the sides
of a well, rising, and falling on afterlives beyond.

F.


And there remains the rampant menagerie
of DSM V out back, that I have done little
about. I used to hunt them on principle.
I wanted to dehorn, neuter them. Debrain
them with air guns. I wouldn't even need
a trophy head to stuff. I'd have returned
them to the elements. But considering
ischemic death distracted from my ischemic
living. And since the beasts are already here,
why not make a bestiary of them? There are
some who would publish these cries for help,
anyway, and critics who would say they are
well-constructed, like newborns drowning
in oxygen and bright sound, crying to everyone's
approval. Applaud my titanic slaps
on the door as I go under. If I am sinking,
I am at least doing it by the meter.


Poetry may be that truce with my death drive,
surrender terms after armies within me reached
Harmagedōn. That the toxins I thus expressed
formed ornate crystals, does not make it art.
This work is to re-pare, make ready with the knife
again. Cruel man that I am, I prefer my singers
broken. No worse than those who like their poets
*fragile, scared*, thrumming with the terror of being
alive. Disentangle my self concept. *The earth will
wear out like a garment* and of my body, *not one
stone will be left upon another*. Perhaps that will
unchain my sin, incarnate and composting,

from my back. Franz Wright (although I should not bother you in repose), saint of men who have reason to hate themselves but find reason to go on, protect me with burly, bastard truths. Urge the necrobiome around me to unionize. Help me arrive beside myself.

I too, am ripening, sibling.
You, who are three-fifths of me, by DNA.
You got that fiber. You got those carbs.
We grew out of shoots hiding desperately ramifying
root systems. When one laden hand wilted,
other offshoots appeared in its place. We have been perennial.
We, reluctant immigrants, have known banana republics,
knew tropics before we were cut
off. Our skins are worse for wear. Mine has been known to almost blanch
in teary drops. Yours, outside the yellowing of ethylene rooms, surrenders
to the encroaching black. I will not insult you by saying this,
how I gorge on you, was a sacrifice. My mouth stays hungry.
Mine were crimes of opportunity, or need.
But if your fingers are mostly water, like mine;
if we are mostly alike, perhaps I was also betraying myself,
replenishing myself,
stocking my losses back,
faster.

I stood at first, thundercatcher, in the rain to see what      shocks might
come; what specters might, passing, be    framed on my plates;
what    whispers in    squall could tell; what gave wronged
fencers    such skill and what    made me, blade aloft to stir the sky,
bait the truth  to guard the house. I'd asked that they remember me
fondly. As parent, I'm little more than chess automaton, battery light
on.      There's a key aloft on a kite,    a copper reel  making its way to
me,      pilot within. I consider oblivion, if it will commute  this
sentience. Current, prompt my motions, or electrocute me. I could
style myself after the renewable  turbines of Sisyphus; mitotic
liver    of Prometheus; or hydro dams of the    river Styx. Something
must awaken    the gyroscope    of my volition. I've heard    that
substances. Unfortunately,         I've also heard that substances.
Perhaps I could learn        from plants. Where's the light? Can I
grow        toward it? Bring me gases to frack,  give me tongued toes to
taste nitrogen and perhaps grow. Give me a way                to make
light  into green lances,    or  windmill slats.      Sabotage my virtual
helmet    and its explosions of pixels      and Dolby sound, into an
electro- convulsive cap    that can wake me up.

I will hide the    armature  of my charging cradle from my children.
I will go to it      at night.

On the planetary probe in search of our origin, we staff the crew with newborns, and hand something of the mission to them. The biological impulse, and love itself, had been simply bulletin boards for shift change. If we are insistently orbital, we must look inward, centripetal and glare-stunned, or outward, center-fleeing, light-tethered, for a reason. *Knowledge will increase.* Each generation will uncover more of the mission from colliders, carbon dating, and thought experiments. Dopamine, oxytocin, and serotonin will be motorcycle helmet foams, adrenaline and cortisol the fossil fuel in the fireplace of doing. *Occupy till I return.* And If you wake on a greenhouse spacecraft losing life support, and older crew cannot tell you why you're there or where you're going, before they die, and your successors themselves hold promises of generations of crew asking the same *why* you can never know, but you look at the photo- and geotropisms of the singular ark terraformed for us, and the tug between that craft and the heavier stars, and the impulse toward gregariousness, and the legacy of destructive agents that might, in spite of themselves, construct a flightplan defiance of the statistical nothing outside, managers who, in their worship of morale, would query the portholes, and seeing only the raven-void winging parsecs past, say there's everything beyond the ark.

For a while I'd needed it bad-bad, my wasness before before-before became now-now. What has follow-follow brought me? And why fear the splintering of self? Anaphoric, reduplicated, moral-injured. I am same. Not. Double-double. Sunned. Zodiac-swung. Zugzwang-stunned. There was a god to encounter on morning walks coincident with dew and the startled hush of dawn. There were trivial acorns of learning in non-trivial pyramids. There is now, the eloquent void. My hair, now uncombed in a little act of self-ownership, a little freedom against owning obligation. Waka-waka. The narrator is always a corrupting influence. The observer is a corrupting influence. The scribe is a corrupting influence. The receiving mind is a corrupting influence. Surely you see it by now: influence is the corruption. When they yearn for what came before, what do they really yearn for? Untombed, resentment is also recursive: presentiment, re-sent kismet. We wanted a home. We took it for granted. We had it crumble. The successive, and then successful, withdrawal of safety. There is no unspoiled past. Fear is the parent-god, the guard tower with the turret guns, the murder hole. Why does nostalgia for a past that left me fractured persist? To discover that *rage is the response of a decorticate animal to stress,* there are scientists who carefully divided mammals from their cerebral cortices, savagely extracted their seething then sacrificed their vessels. If we cannot have a higher-order safety, we must have violence. One must imagine the test subject hangry.

TREMBLING

I: BODY MEMORIES

What does the body
of a disembodied head
remember?

It remembers the gunmetal skin
effaced in fleece. Consider me not,
continent. Let me pass unscathed.

You will see my hands at all times.
The head, in diaspora from its body,
is in another country.

I harbor an exaggerated startle in my flesh—
a scampering of impalas
within the choreography of felled

follicles rising again,
as degloving injuries
dismember me, once more,

from remembering.
Lindsey Graham prays for the natural disaster
that will help him call on the power he believes in,

something eldritch,
with a large capacity to assault enemies.
Gunscopes, consider us not. The hollow-tip dome

has never been far from our heads, anyway.
Due to scheduling conflicts:
beleaguered under the weight

of coalescing laser sights preempting blood,
the machine hum of tinnitus
and the industrial revolutions of the bony gears in my ears;

and cowering
under the vertigo of pestilence:
although I have heard

the petitions of my body,
I have been unable to have this breakdown
until now.


2: SPOON THEORY

Until now,
I had not recognized
the pock marks on my skin

for what they were:
repo marks, tow-tracks
of the earth sampling me

with spoons,
turnstiles of it, forests of it,
as I rhymed my fists

to the grinding of teeth.
Through the amniotic night
before I came here I had practiced

my grip on spoons.
But morning is as it ever was:
The daily egg-and-spoon race,

with my peers racing ahead
while I sit splayed
in the clangor of the starting line.

I have eaten the cutlery of myself
for sustenance. I wear a clatter
of fallen utensils in a skirt around me.

I try not to compare.
but some have spades, river basins,
moon craters to eat their feud.

The Big Dipper
is the center of an expanding porridge.
Little Bear has forgotten the words,

*little pot, stop*, to make it quit.
I have, and am,
a cup of hands,

the ponds of presented cubits
emulating a space for energy to rest,
and persist.

And persist, I have,
Forgive me this survival. When I said:
*My obscurity must now be noticed and no longer ignored,*

I should have said it a little lower, laid a little flower
in the wake of my words.
I now know to fear

the amoral indifference of the food chain;
the strangling-rope song of the forest, the doctrine
of its cigar-cutter jaws, its orchestrated thickets of harm,

its stirrup rootlings waiting to trip, its alarm fruits,
its trees of salted-worm nerve endings transpiring.
Hallowed hallux of the sapient, lead me into heart health.

The children I could have been are on my side,
in the I coming to my aid,
in the no like none other.

Primordial as well,
as in the youth of the world are the whirlpools
of my lizard brain's eyes,

its tails prehensile as sentient flagella.
There must be medicinal ferns nearby as well,
soft for embrace, wanting my safety.

## 4: CONSERVATION | MATTER

There are two oceans embracing within:
the dark ocean gurgles sometimes,
its bulging Coke-can barrels calling to me,

taunting me with their victory
over even teeth built to survive so much.
After the carbonated waves

overrunning pancreas islets,
the flats of acid,
if you revisit the resort by my ocean of regret,

and the clouds are casting revenge down,
risk it all to harvest the bellyup fishes.
Eat them before they turn.


## 5: WEREHOUSE

Turn the corner. In the clearing house where nostalgia
is crated off, forklift operators do not see the fungal bloom
in the corner, taking edges off the picturesque.

Mushroom dreams betray the phantom bodies
they are from. The laser hairs of their fleece heads
spread molten anemone skirts. In the mineral and sepia

throat of the warehouse, a luminescence. Incisors
of insolent usurpers spore unsolicited from obscurity.
Basquiat-crowned lizards must now be noticed, first

in the rapid-moving lifetimes, where nuclear
plumes of old experiments cannot be doused, where no sea
can garrote the thickets of growth that crack the harms

that confined them. Know that solace
had planned, these long nights, to invade, contaminate
the gallons, the irons of your blood, to deliver your exobody,

and its brain, from machines of death. Before you jettison
your anatomy and board a boat, giving shotgun shells for toll,
know that like children, mendings want to song for you.

Trees of non-salted calendar days want to alarm the cruelty
from your broken fingers. They want to sprout herds of fiberoptic
oxen tumbling down. No lance can negotiate their scatter

to find an animal softness. All this begins in the infrared
of the spectrum. There are supply carts there, infusing tropes
of weeklong wings, into the air. The wonder reaches the floor

boards. A jury of pears casts its stones like the grenades
of an invasion. The explosions turn sand into glass barnacles
that erase more of the room. A mouth like this, once incarnate,

stays hungry. So it was that the forklift's snoring passage
picked out that ecology of iridescence.
An invitation to the ones who explain time

with a paper sheet and pencil: Go ahead,
poke holies in my writs of trembling.
And so it was that I awoke with the repressed memory of joy,

having been somnambulant
with one divining-rod arm and one metal-detector, outstretched.
This time, I let the hooves of simple desire stampede

from inevitable corrals. Improbably, the tooth oceans survived
contact with reality. Sleep had woven broken forms around my bite
marks. I carried their fire, letting them warm me, well into the day.

## SECURE ATTACHMENT

1.

At the end of palindromic days,
we perch on our achieved debris.
Not unlike a bird I feed my chick
what she eats well: in this case
scraps of meat, ripping goat corduroy
into short strips. I can't afford this
much of it, but what else can I do?
Later she sleeps so heavy and so long I
check for her breathing, unlike birds do,
I suppose. And all's clear as I resettle
my desk to plot the misery of goats


2.

There is perhaps an absolution
in a toddler going to sleep upon
my chest, in being a major fraction
of her safety, in a 6-year-old seeking
out my heat. In creating, for the first time
in the recorded history of our 4 families,
whatever this is, a security granted for taking.
I have done this right, whatever things
I've also done wrong (and they are many).

## IYÉWÁNDÉ

So I will spoon slop into her mouth.
I will scoop the dribbles from her chin.
I will sponge her down in a warm bath.
I will carry her little body and set her feet on the ground.
I will hold her hand and teach her to walk.
I will tell her what unfamiliar words mean.
I will kiss her on the cheek.

Because for the first six months of her life,
I kept seeing my unmourned grandmother's
face in hers. I am not very fond of ghosts, especially those
I wronged as they turned toward death, coward that I was,
choosing an exile over duty by her bedside
as her ovaries exploded into cluster munitions.
I did not risk my comfort to visit her war.

So I will look in her face tenderly.
I will make the house safe for her.
I will help her discover the world beyond.
I will do things that make her laugh.
I will sit by her bed as she drifts off to sleep.
I will not let her die.

## "IT IS COMMON FOR AN ANIMAL, EVEN IN DEATH, TO RESIST ITS OWN DECONSTRUCTION."

*The animal that therefore I am* wakes daily, prays: *I want, I want, I want.* I want the poem again: poetry as patricide, poetry as effigy-burn; poetry as pen warm against my thigh in swordless alleys; a performance of heresy against warrens of silence; poetry as the medically examined question—the flayed drupe, the flesh disrobed, the extradited, planetary—the stone in a chaos of sluice.

I dare demand the purity of a pain pared down, a pardon from the punishment of eagleform liver biopsies, new every day; internal incantation, anathema incarnate, resolute eternal. I sense my metanoia. *Everything returns, but what returns is not what went away.* I am denuded already but I disrobe, I disrobe, I disrobe again. I deglove layers of the tube I am. I realize now that I do not wish to be repaired. I do not wish to be restored to any previous state. Why would I surrender the slag of loathing, its hardened alloy, the abalone-shell youth fenestrated to light? I'd thought I needed an easier chair, but no furniture could help me feel at ease in the world. I'd wanted quiet, but the noise, the flood is coming from inside my body

But there must be weather at a black hole's mouth, a whistling song at that bottle-rim. I am not masked; I have been entirely made of masks. But now, let me closer to the drain. I want to see what it takes, and what is left. My animal ambulates from the pupa of sleep, the bonds of *no*, the dome beyond, toward the absolution of the dead that cannot forgive me, to the elegy withheld; to be cleansed by the finally burning house of memory I calmly pick keepsakes within, under the darkening blanket and a galactic entreaty of alarms.

## ACKNOWLEDGEMENTS

Earlier versions of some poems in this book appeared in *128 LIT*, *The Ampersand Review*, *Dusie*, *The Fiddlehead*, *trampset*, and *The Tyee*.

I am grateful to CBC Books, and especially Jane van Koeverden, for commissioning "The longing machine," and Ben Shannon for the accompanying illustration.

"Pro-Gnosis," originally published as "Divination," appeared in "Debriding the Moral Injury," a chapter I contributed to the *Routledge Handbook of Medicine and Poetry*. Alan Bleakley and Shane Neilson, eds. (Routledge / Taylor & Francis, 2024).

"Lagos Money" appeared in *African Urban Echoes: A Poetry Anthology*. Jide Salawu and Rasaq Malik, eds. (Griots Lounge, 2024).

I am grateful to:

The Canada Council for the Arts, for grant funding that facilitated the refinement of this work.

The Civitella Ranieri Foundation in Tribeca, New York, and Castle staff in Umbria, Italy for the residency in the desktop-wallpaper-beautiful hills of central Italy. The time, room and board, library, and company the residency provided were magical for my process. I am especially grateful to my cohort of fellows, including Farah Al Qasimi, Catherine Barnett, Shiraz Bayjoo, Reginald Dwayne Betts, Sheroanawe Hakihiiwe, Shawn R. Jones, Salomé Lamas, Jessie Montgomery, Res, Angelica Sanchez, Aart Strootman, Jamila Woods, and Vito Žuraj, and Director's guests Brett Gadsden, Michele Glazer, Lyudmyla Khersonska, Boris Khersonsky, and Natasha Trethewey for their kindness, conversations, and for the gift of their perspectives and feedback as we conversed and collaborated, often across genres.

Aidan Chafe and Bo Joseph for beta-reading earlier drafts of the manuscript. Dorothea Lasky for editing and helping focus a later draft of the manuscript.

Jide Adeyefa, Carl Amouzou, Hope Lauterbach, Rob Taylor, Isabella Wang, Jake Byrne, Olamide Craig, Nick Selig, and Okaima Oyakhirome for personal support that proved key to surviving this book and its preceding events.

Michael Edwards, Andrew French, Daniel Cowper, Kyle McKillop, for workshop feedback that helped many of the primordial poems emerge.

Sincere thanks to Professor James K. A. Smith, Eduardo C. Corral, and Reginald Dwayne Betts for their generous endorsements of this book before it went to press.

I am grateful to Canisia Lubrin, whose incisive editing coaxed this book out from the bloated manuscript I had sent to her. I am also grateful to the rest of the perennially excellent team at McClelland & Stewart for the care with which they have refined and produced this book. Special thanks to Kelly Joseph, Senior Editor; Rebecca Rocillo, Editorial Assistant; Peter Norman, Copyeditor; Stephanie Sinclair, Publisher; Kimberlee Kemp, Senior Managing Editor; Kim Kandravy, Print Producer; Jennifer Griffiths, Senior Designer; Sean Tai, Senior Typesetter; Sarah Howland, Imprint Sales Director; Tonia Addison, Marketing & Publicity Director; and Cameron Waller, Publicist.

I am grateful to my family as well, for sharing me with this affliction.

Àrósò Poetica is a cento of ars poeticas. "Àrósò" is a regionalism for rice from SW Nigeria. Sincere thanks to the authors, publishers, agents, and estates that granted permission to reproduce portions of the source poems. Any errors in composition remain mine. The source for each line, in order, is:

1. "Ars Poetica" by Dorothea Lasky. From *Black Life* (2010). Wave Books.
2. "Ars Poetica" from *The After Party: Poems* by Jana Prikryl, copyright © 2016 by Jana Prikryl. Used by permission of Tim Duggan Books, an imprint of Random House, a division of Penguin Random House LLC. All rights reserved.
3. "Arroz Poetica Battle Rhyme for Kendrick Lamar" by Noel Quiñones. In *Asymptote* (May 2013).
4. "Arroz Poetica" by Aracelis Girmay. From *Teeth* (2007). Northwestern University Press.
5. "An Essay on Criticism" by Alexander Pope (1711).
6. Excerpt from "Bus Stops: Ars Poetica" from *Music for the Dead and Resurrected* by Valzhyna Mort. Copyright © 2020 by Valzhyna Mort. Reprinted by permission of Farrar, Straus and Giroux. All Rights Reserved.
7. 1 line / 6 words / "The Latin Deli" requested from *The Latin Deli* by Judith Ortiz Cofer is being reprinted with permission from the publisher (@1992 Arte Público Press – University of Houston).
8. "How to Be a Poet" by Wendell Berry. From *New Collected Poems* (2013). Counterpoint Press.
9. "Ars Poetica" by Richard Tillinghast. © 2008 Richard Tillinghast.
10. "Ars Poetica with Bacon" by Terrance Hayes. In *The New Yorker* (July 2016).

11. "Epistles Book II and Ars Poetica" by Horace (c. 19–15 BCE). Translated by Ben Jonson (1640).

12. "Poetry" by Claude McKay. From *Harlem Shadows: The Poems of Claude McKay* (1922). Harcourt, Brace & Company.

13. "Ars Poetica as Love Poem with Auto-Correct; or, Mission You" by Perry Janes. From *Find Me When You're Ready* (2024). Northwestern University Press.

14. "Ars Poetica" by Cornelius Eady. In *Plume* (March 2016).

15. Excerpt from "Ars Poetica" from *Promises of Gold* by José Olivarez, translated by David Ruano González. Translation copyright © 2023 by David Ruano González. Reprinted by permission of Henry Holt and Company. All Rights Reserved.

16. "Arte Poética" from *Selected Translations* by W.S. Merwin. Copyright © 2013 by W.S. Merwin, used by permission of The Wylie Agency LLC.

17. Excerpt from "Ars Poetica" from *Zero at the Bone: Fifty Entries Against Despair* by Christian Wiman. Copyright © 2023 by Christian Wiman. Reprinted by permission of Farrar, Straus and Giroux. All Rights Reserved.

18. "Ars Poetica" by Ronna Bloom. From *A Possible Trust* (2023). Wilfrid Laurier University Press.

19. "Ars Poetica" by Primus St. John. From *Communion: Poems 1976-1998* (1999). Copper Canyon Press.

20. "Ars Poetica as the Maker" from *Time Is a Mother* by Ocean Vuong, copyright © 2022 by Ocean Vuong. Used by permission of Penguin Press, an imprint of Penguin Publishing Group, a division of Penguin Random House LLC. Reprinted in the United Kingdom by permission of Jonathan Cape, a division of The Random House Group Limited. All rights reserved.

21. "Ars Poetica: After a Dog" by Patrick Rosal. From *Boneshepherds* (2011). Persea.

22. "The Uses of Poetry" by William Carlos Williams. From *Poems* (1909).

23. Acknowledgment is given to Mary Jean Chan and publisher Faber & Faber Ltd for permission to reproduce a line from "Ars Poetica, XI," as published in *Bright Fear* (2023).

24. "Preamble (A Rough Draft For An Ars Poetica)" by Jean Cocteau. Diligent efforts to find translator information had not succeeded by the time of publication.

25. "Ars Poetica" by Joy Priest. In *VQR* (Spring 2020 / Volume 96/1).

26. "Ars Poetica" by Paul Verlaine. Translated by Norman R. Shapiro. From *One Hundred and One Poems by Paul Verlaine: A Bilingual Edition* (1999). University of Chicago Press.

27. "Ars Poetica" by Orlando Ricardo Menes. In Poets.org. © 2019 Orlando Ricardo Menes. Originally published in *The Southern Review* (Winter 2019).

28. "Ars Poetica #100: I Believe" by Elizabeth Alexander. From *American Sublime* (2005). Graywolf Press. Text reproduced by permission of the publisher, with UK and Commonwealth rights granted by the author's agent on the author's behalf.

29. "Ars Poetica (cocoons)" by Dana Levin. From *Wedding Day* (2005). Copper Canyon Press.

30. "Arse Poetica" by Lucy Tyrrell. In *Bramble* (Wisconsin Fellowship of Poets, Summer 2020). With thanks to the author. Excerpt has been slightly modified, with the author's permission, from the original "becomes the flight of birds."

In **Color Theory,** the whitest white paint (as of when this poem was written) is an extremely opaque acrylic paint called Bright White, invented by Stuart Semple.

In **Come si Dice?** the referenced art pieces are in the ducal palace of Federico da Montefeltro, in Urbino. The marble-inscribed text in the palace courtyard, referenced in the poem, reads in full:

FEDERICVS VRBINI DVX MONTISFERETRI ACDVRANTIS COMES SANCTAE
RO ECCLESIAE CONFALONERIVS ATQVEITALICÆ CONFOEDERATIONIS
IMPERATOR, HANC DOMVM AFVNDAMENTIS ERECTAM GLORIAE
EPOSTERITATI SVAE EXAEDIFICAVIT

QVI BELLO PLVRIES DEPVGNAVIT SEXIES SIGNA CONTVLIT OCTIES HOSTEM
PROFLIGAVIT OMNIVMQVE PRAELIORVM VICTOR DITIONEM AVXIT,
EIVSDEM INVSTITIA CLEMENTIA LIBERALITAS ETRELIGIO PACE VICTORIAS
ARQVARVNT ORNAVNTQVE

The first stanza of **Contronym** owes a debt to Victoria Adukwei Bulley's poem "Declaration" from the collection *Quiet* (Knopf, 2023), a section of which says: "if I live in the belly of the beast, / let me beget sickness in its gut."

In **Discover** ("Our first invention . . ."), the concept of imitative learning is from L.D. Worthy et al., "Uniquely Human," *Culture and Psychology*, Maricopa Community Colleges, 27 July 2020, open.maricopa.edu /culturepsychology/chapter/uniquely-human/. Complex symbolic language: https://www.ncbi.nlm.nih.gov/books/NBK210023/. Opposable thumbs in primates: according to the American Museum of Natural History (AMNH) in New York. "Complex symbolic language" quotes from National Academy of Sciences (US); J.C. Avise and F.J. Ayala, editors, *In the Light of Evolution: Volume IV: The Human Condition*. Washington (DC): National Academies Press (US); 2010. Part III, Cultural Evolution and the Uniqueness of Being Human, https://www .ncbi.nlm.nih.gov/books/NBK210023/. **The Bison Supermarket of the Plains**: "An Ancient Bond with the Land." *Civilization.ca—First Peoples of Canada—Communal Hunters*, Canadian Museum of History, www .historymuseum.ca/cmc/exhibitions/aborig/fp/fpz3b06e.html.

In **Dismantle**, the section title "I drink it up" is a quote from the 2007 film *There Will Be Blood*, starring Daniel Day-Lewis. The "milkshake straw as oilrig pipeline" analogy is from the same film. "Who rightly called us" draws from the quote "The human race is just a chemical on a moderate-sized planet, orbiting around a very average star in the outer suburb of one among a hundred billion galaxies. We are so insignificant that I can't believe the whole universe exists for our benefit. That would be like saying that you would disappear if I closed my eyes," by Stephen Hawking, from a 1995 interview with Ken Campbell on *Reality on the Rocks*: "Beyond Our Ken." "Soma" is from Aldous Huxley's *Brave New World* (Chatto & Windus, 1932). *Noli timere* (Do not be afraid) were said to be Seamus Heaney's last words to Marie Heaney.

In **Ekphrasis,** "Contrafession" takes inspiration from *Deconstruction in a Nutshell*, by John D. Caputo and Jacques Derrida (Fordham University Press, 1996). The concept of circumfession had been an iteration by Derrida, of Saint Augustine's *Confessions*. "Surprising form" and "mechanical ghost" quote from the same book. The concepts of the insistence of god, being vs. may-being, the ghost of god, and the specter haunting all things, as well as the tensions between fidelity and breaking, disruption and attention, are from the same book. I have "become a question for myself" is a quote from Augustine's *Confessions*. **Three Studies for Figures at the Base of a Crucifixion** is the title of at least 2 paintings by Francis Bacon.

**Elegy for the dried bonsai on my balcony** is a concrete poem in the form of half of a bonsai tree in silhouette.

**Emotion Regulation Handout 20A: Nightmare Protocol:** The Nightmare Protocol is a technique for dealing with recurrent nightmares, often in the context of post-traumatic stress. The italicized words at the beginning of each stanza quote from the web page "Nightmare Protocol" on DBTSelfHelp.com (https://dbtselfhelp.com/dbt-skills-list/emotion-regulation/nightmare-protocol/). That web page is in turn modified from *DBT Skills Training Handouts and Worksheets, Second Edition,* by

Marsha M. Linehan. Copyright 2015 by Marsha M. Linehan. "Love may explode the brain's drug lab" owes a debt to the quote "Love is a drug made in the brain" in Sayaka Murata's novel *Earthlings* (Grove Press, 2020) and research findings reported in Stephanie Cacioppo's *Wired for Love: A Neuroscientist's Journey Through Romance, Loss, and the Essence of Human Connection* (Macmillan, 2022).

In **F.**, "fragile, scared" is from the *NYT* Pulitzer profile of Franz Wright: "A Writer Carries On His Father's Legacy of Poetry and Pain," by Danitia Smith, 15 Apr. 2004, www.nytimes.com/2004/04/15/books/a -writer-carries-on-his-father-s-legacy-of-poetry-and-pain.html. DSM V is American Psychiatric Association's *Diagnostic and Statistical Manual of Mental Disorders* (5th ed., 2013). https://doi.org/10.1176/appi.books .9780890425596. *Titanic's* [spoiler alert] Jack Dawson makes an appearance at the end of the first stanza.

The title of **A Famished Road** is a riff off Ben Okri's *The Famished Road*. The austere offices are Robert Hayden's.

**Found in Camus** is a found poem quoting isolated fragments of the Albert Camus essay *The Myth of Sisyphus* (as translated by Justin O'Brien, Vintage Books, 1991; translation originally published by Alfred A. Knopf, 1955).

**Indecision Tree** refers to a fishbone diagram, also called an Ishikawa diagram, used to demonstrate the causes of an event. The structure of the mid-sentence ending was demonstrated in Sarah Vap's *Winter: Effulgences, Devotions* (Noemi Press, 2019).

The title **"It is common for an animal, even in death, to resist its own deconstruction"** is from the novel *Nearshore*, by Jana H-S. *The Animal That Therefore I Am* is the title of a book by Jacques Derrida (Fordham

The prompt for **I was going to buy a parakeet, but the laundromat lost my clothes** was provided by Madeleine Corley.

In **Lagos Money**: *Èkó ò ní bàjé* is the city's motto.

**Lethality:** The formula in the first stanza ($L = \lambda \times W$) is Little's Law, a key formula in operations management. It states that "the average number of items in a queuing system, denoted L, equals the average arrival rate of items to the system, $\lambda$, multiplied by the average waiting time of an item in the system, W." It is described by John D.C. Little in "Little's Law as Viewed on Its 50th Anniversary," *Operations Research* 59:3 (2011), 536–49, https://doi.org/10.1287/opre.1110.0940. The poem also draws some inspiration from "How McKinsey Destroyed the Middle Class," an article by Daniel Markovits in *The Atlantic*, 16 Feb. 2022, www .theatlantic.com/ideas/archive/2020/02/how-mckinsey-destroyed -middle-class/605878/.

The title of **Mating in Captivity** is from the title of a book by Esther Perel, *Mating in Captivity: Unlocking Erotic Intelligence* (Harper Paperbacks, 2017).

The title of **"A mostly private corruption"** is from the Carl Phillips poem "Everything All of It" ("Less by design / than circumstance, my corruptions / have been mostly private") in the collection *Pale Colors in a Tall Field* (Farrar, Straus and Giroux, 2020). Italicized portion is from John Donne's Holy Sonnet 10: "Death, be not proud." *Poetry Foundation*, www .poetryfoundation.org/poems/44107/holy-sonnets-death-be-not-proud.

**The Nigerian "Before Before"** was written after Shane Book's "The Ivorian 'Because Because'" in the collection *Congotronic* (House of Anansi, 2014). A linguistic device explored in the poem is reduplication, commonly found in African languages and creoles. The concept of the eloquent void is from the Albert Camus essay *The Myth of Sisyphus*, which the last sentence also adapts from. "Rage is the response of a decorticate animal to stress" is from one of my old physiology textbooks, although I cannot now remember which one. The concept in turn was from the cruel and unfortunate "sham rage" animal experiments of Walter Bradford Cannon and Sydney William Britton.

**On passphrases stronger than 4 words with 1,000 iterations** quotes from Bhanu Kapil's collection *The Vertical Interrogation of Strangers* (Kelsey Street Press, 2001). Many thanks to Kelsey Street Press for their generosity.

**On whether or not there is marriage in heaven**: in **Septem Peccata Mortalia**, the penultimate stanza was inspired by and partially modified from "I asked if this would all work out / Yes / you said as if you were lying," from the poem "in the middle of predicting my life," in Kelli Russell Agodon's poetry collection *Hourglass Museum* (White Pine Press, 2014). Many thanks to White Pine Press for their generosity. In **Narcissum**, the first stanza contains a modification of the title of Kaveh Akbar's poem in *Poetry Foundation* "Despite My Efforts Even My Prayers Have Turned into Threats." It also quotes from an article about entrapped animals in the website "Exposed Wildlife Conservancy," available here: https://www.exposedwildlifeconservancy.org/news/may-23-update. *"We have crucified our fathers . . ."* is from an earlier poem, "We Are the Pieces of the Things You Did," published in *The Reverie Journal*, Vol. 1 (2015). **Purgatio** makes reference to the title of the Charles Simic collection *A Wedding in Hell* (Ecco, 1994). The phrase "bright and unbearable reality" is a translation of the word "enargeia" in the introduction to Alice Oswald's *Memorial: A Version of Homer's Iliad* (WW Norton, 2013), referring to early reception of the *Iliad*. **Demonstro** quotes from an article by Tibi Puiu, "Just Four Words Capture the Entire Spectrum of Human Emotions in Language," *ZME Science*, 27 Mar. 2024, www.zmescience.com /science/news-science/main-emotional-hubs-langauge/.

**Trembling: Body Memories:** Regarding this subtitle, I was struck by this quote from an interview with trauma therapist Janina Fisher: "For some reason, the amygdala on the right hemisphere side seems to be the center for traumatic memories. What this meant was that we couldn't work with the narrative memory of the event because post-traumatic memories are held as non-verbal feeling and physical reaction memories—what I call body memories." The title of the poem is from that interview. **Spoon Theory:** Spoon theory, developed by Christine Miserandino (who used it to describe living with lupus to her friend), postulates that individuals with chronic health conditions start each day with an allotment of "spoons," or energy units. These units must be disbursed to different activities as the day progresses, and the individual must ration these "spoons" over the course of the day and prioritize according to what they need to do and how much energy they have available that day. Spoon theory has helped individuals with chronic health conditions characterize and manage their energy levels, in view of daily demands on energy stocks that can be lower than those available to individuals without such conditions. Spoon theory is not a description of simple fatigue. My use of it in this poem is as related to mental illness, which like invisible disabilities (that can also include mental illness) can involve dynamics explainable by spoon theory. The phrase "little pot, stop" is from "The Magic Porridge Pot" as recorded by the Brothers Grimm. **Survival Brain:** Bessel A. van der Kolk, author of *The Body Keeps the Score: Brain, Mind, and Body in the Healing of Trauma* (Penguin Books, 2015) said this about the survival brain: "In the long term the largest problem of being traumatized is that it's hard to feel that anything that's going on around you really matters. It is difficult to love and take care of people and get involved in pleasure and engagements because your brain has been re-organized to deal with danger. It is only partly an issue of consciousness. Much has to do with unconscious parts of the brain that keep interpreting the world as being dangerous and frightening and feeling helpless. You know you shouldn't feel that way, but you do, and that makes you feel defective and ashamed." Here is the interview the quote is from: David Bullard, "Bessel van Der Kolk on Trauma, Development and Healing," psychotherapy.net, www.psychotherapy.net/interview/bessel-van-der -kolk-trauma. **Conservation** | **Matter:** An attempt to illustrate the anxiety associated with approaching middle age, and the suspicion that one has not lived as healthily as one needed to. It became garbled with the "there are two wolves" meme, and the Coke ocean metaphor from an earlier series of tweets I should really have saved for a poem.

Sections of several poems are taken or modified from, or are in conversation with, the Bible, including: "A Parable": Acts 16:30; "Contronym": Ecclesiastes 5:2; "Discover": Song of Solomon 8:6; "F.": Isaiah 51:6, Matthew 24:2; "Stigmata": Mark 5:41; "Re-Claim": Job 13:15; "Robber": Luke 8:52; "A mostly private corruption": Ecclesiastes 11:1; "If a day is like a thousand years": 2 Peter 3:8, Psalm 139:16; "I Believe; Help My Unbelief": Mark 9:24; "Para-ambulant": Daniel 12:4, Luke 19:13.

TOLU OLORUNTOBA was born in Ibadan, Nigeria, where he studied and practiced medicine. He is the author of two collections of poetry, *The Junta of Happenstance*, winner of the Canadian Griffin Poetry Prize and Governor General's Literary Award, and *Each One a Furnace*, a Dorothy Livesay Poetry Prize finalist.